MATTER of TIME
KATE O'NEIL

Acknowledgements

Thank you to the many people – family, friends and strangers – whose words or gestures have sparked a thought that became a poem.
Some of these poems have been previously published in collections, magazines and anthologies.
'Scribbly Gums', 'Sunflowers at Wilcannia', 'Hills Hoist', 'Carillon' and 'A Wheatfield, Very Yellow' are included in my Cool Poems reciter, Triple D Books, Wagga Wagga, 2018
Other poems published previously:
'Sondry Folk' in Manchester Metropolitan University's Let in the Stars, 2014
'Lady Cooper, parvenue' in Azuria, Geelong Writers, Winter 2019
'For the Love of Yellow' in Whirlagust, Yaffle Prize Anthology, 2019
'Granny Smith Remembers' in Heroines, Neo Perennial Press, Sydney, 2019 and online
'Miss Bea Miles', 'Occupation: Rebel' in Guide to Sydney Crime, ed. Les Wicks
'Scribbly Gum' in Red Room Poetry: Poem Forest.

Matter of Time
ISBN: 9781761097065
Copyright © text Kate O'Neil 2025
Cover image: Photo supplied by the author
Design by Graham Davidson

First published 2025 by
GINNINDERRA PRESS
PO Box 2 Bentleigh 3042
ginninderrapress.com.au

CONTENTS

Light and Dark
    Light Fingers   7
    Broken   8
    A Wheatfield, Very Yellow   9
    Skylarking   11
    Autumn Chemistry   12
    Lamp   13
    Night Music   14
    Door in the Mountain   15
    Night Wind   16
    Sea Change   17
    Inner Bat   18

Australia
    Sunflowers at Wilcannia   21
    Dust Storm   23
    Red Cedar, *Toona ciliata*   24
    Scribbly Gums, *Eucalyptus haemastoma*   26
    Hills Hoist   27
    Carillon, Sydney University   29
    Brett Whiteley: Summer at Carcoar   31
    Scarborough Cemetery   32
    Bleeding Hearts, *Homolanthus populifolius*   34
    Thunderduck: the Demon Duck of Doom   35
    Turpentines, *Syncarpia glomulifera*   37
    Lady Cooper Parvenue   38
    Granny Smith Remembers   39
    Arthur Stace   41
    'Miss Bea Miles – Occupation Rebel'*   42
    'She's a Fat Tart, Ain't She?'*   44

Words
　　Matter of Time　　　　　　　　　　　　　　　　49
　　Sondry Folk…the condicioun of ech of hem　　50
　　Do Geese See God?　　　　　　　　　　　　　55
　　How to Read Pottery　　　　　　　　　　　　56
　　Enduring Words　　　　　　　　　　　　　　57
　　'Moving Forward'　　　　　　　　　　　　　58
　　Small Change　　　　　　　　　　　　　　　59
　　Press Release　　　　　　　　　　　　　　　60
　　Porpoise Politics　　　　　　　　　　　　　　62

Story
　　Naked Truth　　　　　　　　　　　　　　　　65
　　Strawberry Thief　　　　　　　　　　　　　　66
　　Earthrise　　　　　　　　　　　　　　　　　　67
　　For the Love of Yellow　　　　　　　　　　　　68
　　Spoon Leaves Dish　　　　　　　　　　　　　69
　　The Windmill's Version　　　　　　　　　　　70
　　Canterbury Cathedral 1978　　　　　　　　　71
　　Cannonball　　　　　　　　　　　　　　　　72
　　Persephone's Wedding Diary　　　　　　　　　73
　　Grandfathers　　　　　　　　　　　　　　　　74

Endings
　　Knowing My Onions　　　　　　　　　　　　79
　　My Father's Coat　　　　　　　　　　　　　　80
　　Ripeness　　　　　　　　　　　　　　　　　　81
　　Lesson　　　　　　　　　　　　　　　　　　　82
　　Ghost Town　　　　　　　　　　　　　　　　83
　　Inheritance Memories　　　　　　　　　　　　85
　　Turon　　　　　　　　　　　　　　　　　　　86
　　Come By Chance　　　　　　　　　　　　　　87
　　This Our Exile　　　　　　　　　　　　　　　88
　　After　　　　　　　　　　　　　　　　　　　89
　　Hades　　　　　　　　　　　　　　　　　　　90
　　Departures　　　　　　　　　　　　　　　　　91

LIGHT AND DARK

LIGHT FINGERS

reach above the eastern horizon,
softly lift the dark away,

cross windowsills to beds of sleeping
babies, knowing the way.

Light fingers stroke cheeks, hair,
warm the first moments of day,

tag children in the playground
join the noisy play.

Light fingers soothe at sundown,
beckon beyond the day,

and while they're promising tomorrow,
steal time away.

BROKEN

I do not know
the colour of silence

if it is golden
or not

but words that break it
are all the colours
of the rainbow

that arcs
from broken light

A WHEATFIELD, VERY YELLOW

How beautiful yellow is
said Vincent,
het schildermenneke.*

He saw yellow noon high
over *a wheatfield, very yellow*
and very light,

with a reaper
struggling like a devil
to finish his work.

A small fellow, too,
bent to his task,
but the yellow, by God,
immense.

Yellow radiant and luminous,
and bright like pure gold;
a high yellow note denying
that death in this light
could be sad.

'Ripeness is all.'

And Vincent,
too broken for life outside
gazed through his iron window-bars
struggling to finish
the lightest canvas he had done.

How well Vincent knew yellow –

*yellow whole
and yellow broken up*

Vincent knew

it's *a devil of a question,
yellow.*

Lines in italics are quotations from Vincent's letters.
* het schildermenneke (diminutive): little painter-man (Vincent's nickname)

SKYLARKING

Something's going on in the tall trees
along the bush track.

A cheeky breeze, high overhead,
makes sudden flurries in the canopy
where the treetops hold back
from tagging each other.
Crown-shy, they pattern the sky
like crazed porcelain.

'Can't make us touch,' they tease the breeze,
and tickle the sky instead.

Sunlight, looking down,
sees its chance to play too,
to flicker through a crack,
tag us on the back, vanish again.

The blinking shadows, amazed
at such daring, close their cool ranks
around the peace of deep green,
until bright light ahead, at the end
of the track, shows us the sky,
flat on its back in the lake, laughing.

AUTUMN CHEMISTRY

Don't give me explanations for the colour of the trees;
why in autumn all the leaves turn gold and red,
I'll just watch them riding on the breeze.

Whether molecules, or hormones or a subtle sleight of light,
I'm indifferent to the cause of autumn's hues,
but autumn trees are such a blessed sight.

You've told me all the science but it simply leaves me cold,
while the colours of the autumn are so warm,
blanketing the earth in red and gold.

LAMP

The girl at the piano is playing Liszt.
Gnomenreigen.
Her fingers on the keys perform
intricate spells,
and the tidy rows of hammers
under the open lid
are charmed into wild dance.

But you, poised over her shoulder,
are mesmerised.
Your snake neck, arching down,
is rigid,
so close to hers, unable to strike.
Your bright eye, unblinking,
is spellbound.

The last note dissolves in air,
the gnomes are stilled,
and she turns to you.

'Goodnight,' she says,
her hand soft on your neck
as she switches the darkness on.

NIGHT MUSIC

Birds are hushed as Chopin's nocturne calls
across the garden. Curious stars come out,
and, summoned back, obedient evening falls
and spreads a deepening darkness all about.

The music merges with the sounds of night,
with perfume from night jasmine on the fence
and from the moonflowers, faces staring white.
It works its will, enchanting every sense.

All living things are moved by music's power
to tap the mysteries of time and space.
So Chopin's nocturne at this present hour
brings all nights ever to this present place.

I listen, charmed, until the music ends,
then hear it in the silence it transcends.

DOOR IN THE MOUNTAIN

He told me about the door.
Said he'd wait inside.

I'm looking but I can't find it.
'Straight up from the rockpool,' he said,
'where Bobby Dignam drowned.'

It will be dark soon. I'm frantic.
Below me I can see the rockpool,
but here only lantana and blackberries,
and the escarpment pulling the sun down.
No door.

NIGHT WIND

It's windy, and the night air
carries closer the distant bleat of a goat.
It sounds like your Latifi, but she
died long ago. From the edge of the garden
I can make out, beyond the lit sports-field,
a man walking. It is not you.

More than forty years have gone
since you walked there,
on the track to the rock-pool and the sea,
but tonight in the darkness I imagine
it *is* you, and you're bringing back
oysters and warrigal greens salty as the sea,
salty as the breath of this night's wind.

It's lashing the trees now, whipping up the sea –
time to go in, to shut out these thoughts,
which will not find you here.
I close the door, turn on the light
and see beyond the window
the quivering ghost of my face
still searching the blowing night.

SEA CHANGE

NSW Central Coast

We are not the stuff of legend;
we live small lives
in unremarkable cottages.
Generations before us
lived out their time
in these seaside houses.
We could not have foreseen this.

We know well
the many guises of this sea;
sometimes it is a sidling lapdog,
sometimes a boisterous hound.
Of late it has been threatening,
and tonight it is a raging monster.

Its hunger is loud. Our danger is real.
This sea has designs on us –
its menace intrudes
on mealtime discussions
and anxious phone calls.
Surely a council, deaf for years
to appeals for a seawall,
will listen now.

We clear the table, resolved
to unleash new anger,
to rise up in numbers against
our laggard leaders.

We do not know that tonight,
the sea will do the dishes.

INNER BAT

This little
fly by night
self
folds away
by day,
avoids light
but wakes
in dark
to dreams
of far flight.

While I sleep
shadow psyche
all unseen
wings away
to places I
have never been.

Echoes answer
soundless speaking
ears wide open,
feeling, seeking,
reading the dark.

AUSTRALIA

SUNFLOWERS AT WILCANNIA

Beside the road to Wilcannia,
a solitary sunflower
sings a clear yellow note
tuned true to the bright day,
the round breve of its throat
turned to the climbing sun.

We admire the ardour
of its singular devotion
as we drive on through
endless low grey scrub

until we see them –
a whole burst of sunflowers –
dozens of them
all standing tall
in a triumphal ovation,
the yellow so loud
we are laughing.
Who would have thought it –
here, in this desert place
to hear such praise
from such a congregation?

In perfect unison
they lift their song
into clear blue.

A sense of blessing
stays with us
as we drive on
into more desert
towards the Darling.

There a last
solo flower
sings its antiphon,
the benediction
of amen.

DUST STORM

Air tightens, crouches,
grows red in the face, roars its rage
across plains, paddocks, towns.

Homing cows mouthing the wind,
bite dust and choke.

Red demon-breath conjures its way
through crack and crevice,
past doors and windows slammed against it.
Country living rooms,
cheerful in blue, white and yellow,
become terracotta museums.

Outback life on an ordinary afternoon
is shrouded in apocalyptic gloom,
as red clouds, the weight of paddocks,
ride an occult sky.

Towns and farms gasp
and vanish into thick air.

RED CEDAR
Toona ciliata

Royal Botanic Gardens, Sydney

I have been called
'The tree that built a nation',
an Australian celebrity, an icon.
Generations have sought,
bought and loved
the warm mahogany glow
of my 'red gold',
my beauty rich and rare –
rarer now than ever.

Here in this garden sanctuary
look at me and imagine
tall ranks of my ancestors
standing sentinel
on forest hillsides.

Now they lie in state,
in stately homes,
show-piece chiffoniers,
cabinets, chairs and tables,
finely crafted 'pieces'.
their drawing room elegance
embalmed in beeswax,
the deep, deep red of their age
veiled in lace tatting.

Catalogues of 'Fine Antiques'
publish their eulogies,
lauding their aged patina,
their corbels, their flat pilasters,
acorn finial adornments,
their paterae, and,
without irony,
their foliate carvings.

SCRIBBLY GUMS
Eucalyptus haemastoma

Tall custodians of scribbled mysteries,
What can you tell us, silent trees?
What tunnelling scribes find sanctuary
within this covert library?

Mere larvae, small but diligent,
whose little lives are wholly spent
to leave these ciphers in your care
till later times reveal them there.

What is the urgent need that drives
this tracery of transient lives?
What are the messages layered here
in darkness? Why, year after year

do you allow these prophets in?
Is there an itch beneath your skin?
Are you, tall gums, merely content
to give their need your nourishment?

Or do your lives and theirs conspire
to keep these riddles from our eye
till when these poets take their leave,
you wear their heartsongs on your sleeve?

The scribbly gum is a eucalyptus tree with a very smooth, pale trunk. The distinctive brownish 'scribbles' are made by the larvae of the tiny scribbly moth.

HILLS HOIST

Broken now,
and waiting for council clean-up
it remembers 1946
and the pride of Lance Hills,
how it stood centre stage
under a sunny spotlight
and became Monday's mecca,
monument to washdays,
how, steady as a beacon
it marked the end
of the backyard's concrete aisle
and how,
next to Sunday's godliness
its own wide arms
flaunted white-as-snow cleanliness,
rising triumphantly
to whirl in the drying wind
and bless us all with
sun-fresh sheets at night.

That joyous wheeling
stirred our childhood dreams
of revolution
to dizzy limits
and midweek rebellion.

Defying rules,
we spun in noisy orbits
past the four corners
of our known flat world.
Suspended by our hooked knees,
hair tumbling earthwards,

faces reddening masks,
we imagined wings and flight.

Sheer carnival
those madcap moments spent
down-under
upside-down.

CARILLON, SYDNEY UNIVERSITY

Sunday afternoon,
and there's stillness
in the university,
its square stone heart
a measured space
of cloistered quiet –
a place apart
from the fevered city,
arteries hectic with
blare and clog
of traffic.

Here history lies
resting in peace
beneath the clocktower,
marking time
until the hour
when sudden bells
ring out resurrection.
Listen, wake, rise,
feel jubilation,
feel alive.

Ring bells, ring.
Renew. Revive.

This is music for the world,
set free to play in treetops,
to wrap around buildings,
to creep through
chinks in traffic,
to weave its way
where it will

and after,
in the silence,
to keep on ringing
still.

BRETT WHITELEY: SUMMER AT CARCOAR

Cool through the summer yellow,
the river parts the dry land,
bends and binds,
winding away then back,
its paint strokes defiantly
taking it to the top of the frame.

You understand spaces by their edges,
their divisions,
their inclusions.

Here poplars stretch up,
creatures burrow or fly
beside the curve of river,
while a dash of black highway
hoons in mimicry
across the top corner
and out.

SCARBOROUGH CEMETERY

Death is untidy here on this clifftop,
its drop sheer as an ending.
Slip-land groans and gapes
under the weight of the stone huddle.

Below, the ocean knocks,
relentless, merciless,
shuddering the sleepers
in their tossed, disordered beds.

Dreams, loosened from their heads,
are snagged on wind-bent, twisted trees.
Weeds claw from cracks in tilting tombs,
headstones bow in defeat.

A rope of root tethers the tomb
of John, son of June, dearly missed,
like the apron strings, the clipped wings,
the resentment that took him.

Thomas, 'accidentally killed by a bullock',
didn't think of death at all
as he vaulted over the boundary fence,
late, on the quick way home.

Gloria, single and childless,
tilts beyond the northern boundary,
towards the preschool playground,
and the sound of laughter.

Here, time wins over history.
Weather erases the stories,
landslip and wind-sweep
slowly inter the graves.

BLEEDING HEARTS

Homolanthus populifolius

A pioneer species

Along the creekbank
they signal their convictions
most intensely
when backlit by afternoon sun.

They have known rising and setting suns,
empires and colonies;
they know every moment is a beginning
under a circling sky.

Their pioneer spirit recalls
an earlier time reminding us
that the stain of blood recurs
through the history of this country.

But these red hearts also speak
of warm-blooded love,
falling in age, preparing the ground
for new life in barren places,

wardens of the dream of generation,
breeding in the deep litter
of their protective nursery,
the forests of time to come.

THUNDERDUCK: THE DEMON DUCK OF DOOM

An extinct Australian flightless bird

Thunderduck's a dead duck –
hear his tale of gloom.
He's dead just like the Dodo,
this Demon Duck of Doom.

Bullockornis planei
(Thunder's other name)
was something of a whopper
but died out just the same.

He weighed two hundred kilograms
and stood two metres high –
sometimes even bigger –
and no, he couldn't fly…

which meant he was a sitting duck
when he went to drink
at the inland waterholes
for, lurking near the brink,

were very hungry crocodiles
who liked the taste of duck
and quickly made a meal of him –
such was Thunder's luck.

A flightless duck's a lame duck
and lame things disappear
according to Charles Darwin,
so he's no longer here –

not fit for survival,
and so, to be succinct,
Thunderduck is history;
defunct, bygone, extinct.

Yes, Demon Duck's a dead duck;
dead as dead can be.
You'll never see a Thunderduck
or have one cooked for tea.

TURPENTINES
Syncarpia glomulifera

These trees, these tall turpentines,
have taken years to push back so much sky.

When houses first sidled up to their green shade,
they were already interceding with the heavens,
spreading their sheltering branches
wide in invitation.

Then, when the houses themselves grew
and jostled for elbow room,
the turpentines were resented,
declared too big, unsuitable.
Qualified landscape gardeners suggested
small trees,
shrubs,
ground covers,
architectural grasses.

They spoke knowledgeably of
variety of form,
balance,
harmony –
knew the texts available in the local library –
an air-conditioned refuge
from Saturday morning's discordant noise
of blower vacs and lawnmowers.

LADY COOPER PARVENUE

Karl von Scherzer to Lady Cooper*

It's been a treat to meet you, Lady Cooper,
I see your reputation's well-deserved.
The splendour of your mansion's overwhelmed me
to the point where I am feeling quite unnerved.
I thank you, Madam, that you took the trouble
of showing me your treasured chinaware
and assure you I will not forget the story
of the carvings on the wall behind the stair.

Sir Daniel's presence in the colony
reminds us of the seats of English style,
and serves to make us all reflect upon
the higher culture of the 'sceptr'd isle'.

You say it's time for croquet on the lawn?
Oh, pardon me, so rude of me to yawn.

* Karl von Scherzer (1821–1903) was an Austrian economist, ethnologist, and later consular official. Extract from his Australian Novara Diaries, 30 April 1857–26 August 1859:
'Sir Daniel Cooper lives in most elegant, almost princely style, but one is immediately aware of being in the house of a parvenu. Great efforts are made to imitate certain social conventions, but they miscue all the time and their lowly origins are obvious everywhere. This is particularly the case with the female members of the household, Lady Cooper etc. One is most dreadfully bored in spite of all the delicacies that are served and the treasures that are shown to visitors, and I let out a long yawn when we at long last drove away from Rose Bay.'

GRANNY SMITH REMEMBERS

They are hard things, death and winter.
I'd known too much of both in the Old Country.
Eight babes I brought to birth;
three did not wake to the light.
Grief wintered in me,
settled there like English damp.

We came to this place
for a new life,
chancing the unknown.

I was looking, that morning, for small things,
need aching in me
for the lifting of winter's weight,
for the hope spring brings.
Wanting signs.

I looked into the new day
the way the eyes of the drowning
scan the vastness
for the smallest of specks.

And saw it.
A little pippin –
sole green thing reaching for light
from the dark of the refuse heap,
the cast-out waste
from some French crab apples.

One little pippin.

I'd known loss,
the cruel cuts of chance,
but I'd known defiance too,
and my heart leapt to find it here.

Seedlings keep the secret of their fruit
until it's seen;
there would be years to wait,
but I saw the pippin's resilience,
whatever it might become.

I'd tend this tree, lovingly,
and chance the apple.

'The Granny Smith, also known as a green apple or sour apple, is an apple cultivar that originated in Australia in 1868. It is named after Maria Ann Smith, who propagated the cultivar from a chance seedling.' – Wikipedia

ARTHUR STACE

Wherever Stace was moved to walk
he used the transience of chalk
to celebrate Eternity,
the greater vision he could see
beyond the limits of his time –
beyond his world of guilt and crime.

His vision was an afterlife
where all he knew of earthly strife
would be transmuted into love
flowing from a God above.
For him a saving message stirred
within his single chosen word.

And now, engraved inside a bell
Arthur Stace's script will tell,
the sacred story he once heard,
contained within that single word.
The silent bell will have its say
and speak long after Arthur's day.

and though his human voice is dumb,
his word will sound till Kingdom come.

Arthur Malcolm Stace (1885–1967), an eccentric known as Mr Eternity, was an alcoholic who converted to Christianity and began inscribing the word 'Eternity' in copperplate writing with yellow chalk on footpaths around Sydney, from 1932 to his death. The story of his life has inspired books, museum exhibits, statues, an opera, and a film.

'MISS BEA MILES – OCCUPATION REBEL'*

I'd always known authority
was up to no good,
but after my fever I knew that I should
do something about it.
Society needed a wake-up call,
and I, a 'true thinker and speaker'
would give it my all.
It was my dream job – 'Rebel'.

I could not stand 'the hypocrisy, lies, pretence,
conventional speech and behaviour
upon which society is based'.
So priggish. So strait-laced.

So I rebelled as I felt I ought –
kicked against the 'rules' I was taught.
Wore a ballgown to ride a man's bike
(behaviour 'decent folk' didn't like) –
sometimes tennis shade and shoes,
an army greatcoat when it was cold.
Did what I liked, said what I thought.
Spent a lot of time in court.

For four years I was put away –
my father's 'authority' holding sway,
till the Smith's Weekly journalists
heard of my plight,
and knowing I was in the right,
argued the case to have me freed.

Authority's often in the wrong –
the lawyers, the judges, and the police -
they are the ones that breach the peace.

I felt compelled to speak my mind –
I was rational – I'd been certified 'sane'.
My arguments were clear and plain.
I spoke the truth when I told the court
the arresting officer's report
was seriously lacking in honesty,
and his grubby case should be opposed.
I insisted my bloomers were not exposed
until he pulled my blanket off.

And charged with smoking next to a sign
saying, Gentlemen requested not to smoke,
my gender defence wasn't merely a joke.

The prime minister wasn't as famous as me,
but just like him, I preferred
to get around the place chauffeured.
I became a legend, riding free
on taxis and buses – no ticket for me.
a ratbag, a rascal, the eccentric Bea.

* The Australian Women's Register

'SHE'S A FAT TART, AIN'T SHE?*

In the Spiegeltent, at a sell-out concert
starring Madam Pat Thompson,
'big blues belter', and her 'Orkestra',
the boys begin to play.

The audience hushes
but knows it hasn't started
till the fat lady sings.

A wheelchair brings her on.
She climbs on her stool, centre stage,
and ignores embarrassed whispers
at the awkwardness of her arrival:
this is her place now, she'll show them.

She'll wrap her audience in love,
give them the songs they need,
'He's Funny That Way', Miss Otis Regrets',
'Boulevard of Broken Dreams',
freeing the primal scream. Releasing and saving.
She's done this for twenty two years now.

She lifts her face – she's shining –
and with outstretched arms
Madam Pat, eighty-four,
begins to sing the blues.

'Belt it out, big fat red-hot mamma,'
a voice calls,
'Honey, you should've been born black.'
and Madam Pat smiles at the compliment.

The whispers stop.
She knows she has them now.
Her memories of passion and loss, of all her lives
from shearer's cook to legendary blues performer,
fire the soul in her songs,
sentimental, raunchy, comical, joyous.

All the world's in this tent,
as the fat lady sings.

Pat Thompson is a legend on the south coast of NSW, a cabaret star in Australia and Europe, and the Grand Madam of The Famous Spiegeltent. Her musical career spanned a history of musical styles, performers, and venues from the Melbourne Tivoli in the 1920s to the Edinburgh Festival and Parisian jazz cellars in the 1980s, to her last performance, at 84, in The Famous Spiegeltent in 2008. (ABC 9-part documentary 2012.)

* Comment made by Madam Pat Thompson's future father-in-law when he first met her. It became the title of her autobiography.

WORDS

MATTER OF TIME

I'm reading a letter from you
from a long gone age.
Strange how the edifice of stacked years
implodes in a moment –
how you, unthinkably dead,
can emerge present and living,
your voice so clear,
from the sere, the yellow page.

SONDRY FOLK...THE CONDICIOUN OF ECH OF HEM

Chaucer – Prologue to The Canterbury Tales

Blatherskite

Even though it's utter blather,
soaps his talk into a lather –
spreads it round with open slather.

Hear the wordy-gurdy guy
spinning all his words to 'I'.

Curmudgeon

What a grizzly, grouchy grumper,
glaring, swearing table-thumper.
The world is there to grumble at.
The world is mad! And that is that!

Dandiprat

This man, he's small.
Talks small. Acts small.
Hard to please
this mini-cheese.
Can't think big at all.

Fustilugs

Who is this almighty guzzler,
grasping, grabbing, gross and greedy?
All she does is sit and gobble!
Not surprised she looks so seedy.

Haggersnash

'You'll keep. Just you wait.
You'll regret it's you I hate.'

A haggersnash must do his worst
to hurt because he 'feels hurt first'.
Watch him tend his little rancour
till he has a good-sized canker.
Things are looking really grim –
the canker's almost swallowed him!

Mumpsimus

He knows his mind.
He shuts it tight.
He will not budge.
He will not bite.
He has no doubt.
His way is right.

Nazzard

'Living life is such a hazard.
Excuse me while I stay away…
You will not miss a lowly nazzard.
I'll take my ball and leave the play.'

Quodlibetarian

First he argues back and forth,
then argues to and fro
and when there's nothing more to say
he argues anyhow.

Scobberlotcher

What an idle layabout!
Likes to loll in lotus land.
Need a worker? Count him out.
He has a long siesta planned.

Sneckdraw

This guy's act is hard to beat.
He's the master of deceit –
a slippery, sneaky little cheat!

Only someone of his kind
could understand his devious mind.

Tatterdemalion

Where'd ya get the glad rags baby?
That gear has sure seen better times.
Was that velvet in its heyday?
And on your legs – were they once jeans?
Those shoes might once have had some glamour;
(Perhaps when Elvis was alive)
That whiff! That drift! That faint aroma!
Is it Mildew No 5?

Quockerwodger

'Up down.
Left right.
Yes Sir.
Black's white.
You bark.
I'll bite.'

Wallydrag

This guy's utterly inutile.
Everything he does is futile.
I'm sorry for the wallydrag.
Who'd choose to be a worthless rag?

Whiffler

Will he? Won't he?
He doesn't know.
Can't work out
which way to go.
It could be 'Yes'
but might be 'No'.
The whiffler whiffles
to and fro.

Windlestraw

He's tall and gaunt
and very thin.
So weak and worn
he's mostly skin.
A wind'll sure-
ly do him in.

DO GEESE SEE GOD?

reflections on a palindrome

It sure must get a gander's dander
if his goose with airy 'candour'
says she sees the deity –
a gift denied the laity
of every other feathered soul –
most unlikely on the whole.

And yet they show one-up-man-ship
and feel it is their right to nip
those other birds who aren't 'the best';
those whose eyes are not so blessed.

Has something deep within them stirred
the sense they are the bird preferred
above the duck or swan or hen?
Is their honk a loud 'amen'?

Do geese see God? And if they do,
is it a front or backward view?

HOW TO READ POTTERY

Know your commonness
as human clay. Think how pliable,
how impressionable you were
when new to existence.

Take the finished pot.
Imagine it as clay, soft and formless
on the potter's wheel.
Imagine it turning, rising, falling,
beginning again.

Feel the heat of the kiln,
the glaze realising its shine,
its colour.
Feel the attention of the hands
that first held it
cool and finished.

No. Unfinished.
You hold it now and will change it.
You are the reader meeting the text,
holding the meaning between you.

This hard copy
contains its soft beginning,
remembers the heat.
Begin to read.

ENDURING WORDS

Words endure longer
than the places where they fall.

The stair carpet where I protested
at his muddy footprints is long gone;
its replacement needs replacing.

But those words were made to last.
'Well, clean it, it's your job.'

Perhaps they had already endured –
and been endured.
Perhaps they were inherited words.

'MOVING FORWARD'

Let's celebrate the future we are moving forward to.
It's out there, bright and shining, after all that we've been through.

The world is all before us – 'the best is yet to come'.
What has the past to offer us? Looking back is dumb.

What can we learn from fossils? From digging up the past?
What use are all those ancient texts? We're moving forward – fast.

Why read those dead white poets, and other writers too?
They're obsolete, outmoded – we only need what's new.

We're kicking off from history (no backstroke – that's too hard).
We'll all be swimming overarm, and won't be caught off guard

by bumping into obstacles like superseded facts.
There's no end to the arguments that kind of thing attracts.

So Forward's where we're going – we've seen the light ahead –
we've put the policies in place to put the past to bed.

The arts will only drag us down – they're fiscally defunct.
'Growth' and 'progress' rule the day – dreaming's been debunked.

It's Forward! Ever Forward! Get moving! You will find
a Brave New World is coming. So don't be left behind.

SMALL CHANGE

is a threatened species,
belittled, derided.

Pockets, their linings intact,
don't even mourn it,
the chink of small change
is a fading memory.

Once, in its heyday,
it fed piggy banks,
paid for ice cream or coffee,
celebrated lost teeth.
You could count on small change.

Coin purses were fat with it,
some lived in jars, or on shelves.
Some slunk off behind sofa cushions,
under car seats, down drains.
Some took chances in wishing wells,
or sought immortality in albums.
Hoping.

Electronic monetary transactions
have meant a big change
for small change.

PRESS RELEASE

Bertie was a 'Bear of Note',
known as a VIB;
better than a common bear,
as Bert himself could see;

He was the perfect shade of brown
with nothing to be seen
of scruffiness or matted bits.
He was muscly and lean.

Bertie Buzzwig's pedigree
was evident to all.
Bertie made quite sure of that;
he made a daily call

to someone at The Bruin Mail
who earned a handsome wage
for every breaking Buzzwig tale
that made the social page.

The tales he told were very tall,
so used up lots of space,
and every tale was underneath
a shot of Bertie's face.

So Bertie was a megastar –
every move he made
was closely watched by Everybear
to many an accolade

until he met a foreign Bear
whose coat was honey pale
and Bertie somehow fell for her
and thereby hangs the tale

of Bertie and the Twist of Fate
that saw his fortunes turn –
for Honey was the kind of bear
The Bruin Mail would spurn.

Honey had a certain style,
an independent streak;
she scorned the Bruin journos
and so, within a week,

Buzzwig found himself adrift –
cut from the social scene,
for there he found his Honeybear
was deemed a drama queen.

And so together, hand in hand,
They went to live, 'unseen'
by prying, unkind, gossip bears,
a life on the silver screen.

PORPOISE POLITICS

A Porpoise with a purpose proposed a promenade
along the pebbled pavement – a peaceable parade

to publicise some problems that planning might appease,
and plead for proper practice in porpoise policies.

A perspicacious pamphlet pointedly professed
that persistent use of plastic was perturbing. So they pressed

for a pause in its production, and the porpoise parson prayed
for the plan to be perfected by employees who'd be paid.

'Plastic is pollution' a pennant proudly preached
(and opponents of this project should promptly be impeached.)

In part, they planned a purging of porpoise politics.
The protest was persuasive and a press report predicts

that persistence in promoting these proposals will procure
the populace's preference for a planet that is pure.

The porpoise politicians pondered their position
perused the prescient paper and proffered their permission.

A porpoise was appointed to specifically preside
over practical precautions and personally provide

protection for the project. Pikers who'd complain,
and were petulant or peevish, would promptly feel the pain

of publicised opprobrium; a penalty for spite
and plots that would perpetuate the porpoise planet's plight.

STORY

NAKED TRUTH

She came to the party with no trace of shame,
and though she was naked, strode in just the same.

Everyone knew her – but all turned away –
embarrassed to see this outrageous display.

They averted their eyes, inspected the floor,
needed the loo, or made for the door,

just as a latecomer sauntered in.
Gasps of confusion – Did Truth have a twin?

Truth stood her ground looking face to face
with Falsehood, who, to her disgrace

was wearing Truth's clothing – her own left behind,
at the pool where they'd swum, and where she'd designed

a cunning swap (with mischief in mind) –
a plan which Truth at once declined.

Refusing to wear any clothes but her own,
she'd come as she was to the party, alone,

knowing at least she'd cast doubt on the lies
that Falsehood might spread in her stolen disguise.

STRAWBERRY THIEF

a William Morris design

Beady-eyed, the bird spies ripe berries,
red treasure amongst the green leaves.

There must be other strawberry thieves,
but this bird is famous
for his filching.

See him there, berry in beak,
face to face with his sleek reflection.
He's caught in the act
on wallpaper, a Liberty print,
trinkets by the score.
Could you need more proof?
Recorded on repeat,
this theft's a fact. The Truth.

Or is it?
He's called a thief
but are we deceived?
The berry, so temptingly sweet,
so tantalisingly close,
is never enjoyed by the bird –
the perfect berry, forever unspoiled,
is always only almost thieved.

EARTHRISE

Familiar places, like childhood,
are seen with new eyes
when we look back;
to be close, is to be blind
to the distant view.

The gravity-pull of the heart
does not change
as the flat earth of childhood
becomes the round spinning world
we learn to know,
the long distances of
the Globe we travel.

But the vision of the
whole wide onlooking world
is transfigured
when Bill Anders,
from the outside, looking on,
shows us a small blue marble
rising over the moon.

And America celebrates
Earthrise
on a postage stamp.

FOR THE LOVE OF YELLOW

They are so many, the shades
and mysteries of yellow.
Sunshine, light,
ripeness and sunflowers.
Autumn leaves, old paper.

And, in my birthday paint-set
of tiny oil-paint tubes,
I find this: Naples yellow.

It's love at first sight.
Years later I am still drawn to it.

It is yellow's down time.
Serene. Quiet. Opaque.
The underside of a just-hatched chicken.
Wraps you in baby blankets.
Indulgent as clotted cream.
Safe, comforting yellow.

Until I discover its history,
learn that it is toxic
and expensive.

Like much I have found magnetic.

SPOON LEAVES DISH

I liked him at the time –
thought he was quite dishy
when we ran away.
But no,
I couldn't stay
with someone so wishy-
washy. His get-up-and-go
got up and went.
And so did I. Ran away again.

This time teamed up with
a right mug.
Too strait-laced for me.
I was bouncing off the walls.

Being a bit of a stirrer
I told him I'd fallen
for a cauldron –
dark, handsome, mysterious…
and I was off again.

But the truth was,
I needed a break.
I missed hanging out
with my friends
and headed
back to the drawer
for a group hug.

THE WINDMILL'S VERSION

We were just doing our thing –
an easy, lazy, up-and-over spin of our arms
in a mild wind,
when this loon came out of nowhere,
screaming blue murder.

We heard a horse too,
a sad, strained gallop,
and saw the flash of a sword.

The codger roared like one possessed
as he charged straight at us,
calling us 'evil giants'.

He hit my sail at full tilt
and up he went – up, over
and down
like a swatted mosquito.

I thought I'd finished him.
How could I know an impossible dream
would raise him to greatness –
that we'd be known ever after
as 'Don Quixote's windmills'
living on here
for hundreds of years,
straddling the skyline like giants?

CANTERBURY CATHEDRAL 1978

Our arrival by car is not the pilgrim's way
and no one is telling stories,
but lines from Chaucer's Prologue
repeat in my mind.

Whan that Aprill with his shoures soote
The droghte of March hath perced to the roote,
And bathed every veyne in switch licour
Of which vertu engendred is the flour…
Thanne longen folk to goon on pilgrimages…

Chaucer's pilgrims came to revere the hooly blisful martir;
we have come to see the grandeur of this many-storied stone.

The crush of centuries takes my breath away
and I creep outside to resume my single day.
It's quiet behind the cathedral, and warm in the sunlight.
I sit beside a solitary weed
trailing from a crevice,
its green startling the stone;
its time brief as an April shower.

History won't record or care
that we were there together,
in 1978,
ephemeral and small.

CANNONBALL

excavated near *The Rose Elizabethan playhouse*

This ragstone ball,
shaped centuries ago
for warfare,
did it, in its time,
see active service?
Did it hear the noise of battle
made distant by the one
deafening moment of its own
explosion onto the scene?

Or did it avoid conflict,
with a more peaceful casting in Special Effects,
faking thunder
at the Rose playhouse,
serving its time as
Thor's pretender in The Tempest,
King Lear, Macbeth,
rolling across the timber slats
of 'The Heavens' floor?

PERSEPHONE'S WEDDING DIARY

Mother had something against him –
said he gave her the shivers
and no way could I be his wife.

But he had his ways and
tbh I was swept off my feet.
He can be charming.

This new darkness
makes my heart race. Fear?
Excitement? I'm not sure.

But the wedding was sensational.
He went all out with the revels
in the glow-worm caverns.

Flame-light danced in our eyes
at the feasting, and oh,
that pomegranate salad.

GRANDFATHERS

1 Aradale (Daniel)

And (Noah's) ark rested…upon the mountains of Ararat. – Genesis 8:4 KJV

They called it a sanctuary,
a place of refuge,
asylum.

Here the sad, the insane, the suffering,
were rounded up and stored.

Those whose concern it was
to seek out the homeless,
the disorderly, the uncooperative,
were there for my grandfather.

They saw him drowning,
brought him in, struggling,
from the churning streets,
and landed him high and dry
in Aradale.

Aradale Asylum was a psychiatric hospital, located in Ararat, a rural city in Victoria, Australia. Now a ghost town, Aradale was once known as the Ararat Lunatic Asylum.

2 Inheritance (James)

'Who do you think you are?'
my grandfather asks
when he catches me running
through his house.
He doesn't see Bobby chasing me.

I don't answer him, knowing
nothing will stay his hand.
Not even Nanna, who would if she could.
It's for my own good,
he says,
he's not sparing the rod

Frail in his 80s, he's living in our house now.
The smacks he gave me then are nothing
to the tongue-lashings he gives himself
at night, weeping, remembering, praying.

He's sleeping near my room, cursing himself
as if his father's curses weren't enough.
'You killed your brother.'
and memory, on repeat, is killing him.

He's six. Michael, two, is standing in his cot,
asking to get out and play. My grandfather
helps him out, and Michael, in flannel gown,
runs too close to the fire.
His death endures for generations.

ENDINGS

KNOWING MY ONIONS

I prepare
their bed with care,
sow the seed
lovingly,
wish them well,
draw over them
a soft blanket of loam.

I attend to every need:
give them water,
composted feed,
encouraging words.
Sometimes a poem.

I praise the spring green
of their first shoots.
I watch them grow.
They are my onions;
I know them well.

I know one day
they will bring me to tears.

MY FATHER'S COAT

Those cold winters chilled me to the bone;
shivering in bed, nothing made me warm
until my father covered me with his coat.

The comfort of its weight kept out the cold
and, warm at last, I'd curl cocooned in sleep
beneath the cover of my father's coat.

My father's gone. The coat went long ago;
I thought I'd never know of warmth again
the moment when I saw my father cold.

RIPENESS

When the flare of summer
dims, days shorten
and the air cools to mist,
there is still much to come.

Autumn brings fruition,
the garnering of grist
to be stored in rhyme.
Autumn presages
the fullness of time.

Late sun is amber,
pouring gold
across the garden;
the story almost told.

LESSON

The backyard where I dreamed
was a square of green lawn,
enclosed by paling fences.

Supine at its centre,
I'd look up at the whirling clouds,
the arch of heaven reeling over me,
declining to be the firmament
described in the Lesson

The ground felt firm beneath me
as I lay there,
my body rehearsing even then,
its human death,
which, according to Sundays,
was the only way I'd fly.

GHOST TOWN

welcomes careless drivers

We don't mind what brings you here –
rage or speed. That extra beer
might be to blame. All the same
the thing that matters is – you came.

'Stay, stay, don't go away,'
you'll hear ethereal voices say.

No matter how you met your fate,
our hospital's hospitality's great.
It's here you'll wait while you have breath,
and hesitate to meet with Death.

But if they find you silent and still
you'll have to wait in the morgue until
they've sorted out your shroud and tomb
and organised your underground room

in the nearby graveyard. Here you'll meet
the bods with whom you'll trick or treat,
haunt or spook (you'll learn the rules) –
poltergeists, and ghosts and ghouls,
spirits and spectres.

      And just in case
Ghost Town's Senior Spirit of Place
should find you shirking, he explains
you'll find yourself in clanking chains
that weigh your weightless being down
and trace your passage through the town.

This Spirit's proud of Ghost Town's fame –
how well it hosts the haunting game –
so while the welcome is sincere,
Terms and Conditions are quite clear.

INHERITANCE MEMORIES

When I go

I'd like to leave you memories of spaces
so vast you'll see how little you can see:

the ocean reaching past your far horizon –
you'll never fathom all its mystery.

The wide red plains that seem to stretch forever
from mountains westward to the setting sun.

the endlessness of starlit skies at midnight,
which tells of distant spaces known to none.

And that vast universe of books and reading
where you'll glimpse worlds of others from afar.

I'd like to leave you memories to lead you
to understand how small we humans are.

TURON

Your death confounds
the linear ways of time
which eddies round me,
in swirling memories,
sometimes warm, sometimes cool,
like the drifts of river shallows,
which are not keeping up
with the river.

Memory calls up a single day,
clear as a photograph,
when we waded in the Turon River
in shallows like this,
imagining dreams could
pull time aside too.

In those pooled hours
we thought we saw a lifetime

but the sun rose higher
while beyond the shallows,
the river flowed.

COME BY CHANCE

We'd laughed at the name of the town –
'Come-by-Chance',
but didn't go there. Ever.

But I came by chance once,
in a book randomly opened,
on a poem dedicated to you.

And now, by chance, I find
your funeral streamed online.

White-knuckled, I watch your life
in a slide show. There you are,
you, in my garden,
my goat in your arms.

Then, one by one, your later ghosts
file by; all I will ever know
of a life I didn't live.

THIS OUR EXILE

Since I last saw you
I have always thought of you
as alive, somewhere
on this same planet.
That comfort has gone.

I hope you laughed a lot.
I hope there were long stretches
of contented outback days,
tea in the pot, herbs in the garden,
dogs.

Tonight I held your rosary
with its one-armed Christ,
and wept.

AFTER

They've closed the brackets now,
around the time that was yours.
These hard curved ribs,
mere punctuation, hold you
fixed in time and place;
a name and numerals.

Don't let them do that.

Let them be boat ribs,
of a vessel taking the whole man,
fully made, finished,
through the essential dark
the living can't know,
to a spring stirring in myths.

HADES

I drew the short straw.
Darkness. Cold. Earth.
This was my life.
And yet, it had its attractions -
a kind of serenity. 'Peace and quiet'
should not be under-rated.
I know.

I remember the agitation, the turmoil
I felt when I saw her.
Persephone.
I lost it. Her beauty undid me
completely. I behaved badly.
Things were unsettled for some time
after I made her mine.
She missed the green world. The flowers.
She was unhappy.

And the mother! Spare me that!
We couldn't go on like this.

Compromise. It came to that.
She returns to her world for a time.
But then comes back to me.
And she brings a new hope,
a feeling of potential,
something biding its time.

DEPARTURES

The mirror path we're walking
will be gone soon,
ephemeral boundary
between sand and receding tide.

Along this swath of blank wet shine,
light focuses on small things;
breath bubbles of burrowed sandcrabs,
filigree foam, underwater clouds,
all fleeting,

sucked away
with the forgiven sins of our footprints,

leaving no trace.

www.ingramcontent.com/pod-product-compliance
Lightning Source LLC
Chambersburg PA
CBHW071910070526
44583CB00016B/1920